JavaScript Programming

*A Complete Guide For Beginners To Master
And Become An Expert In JavaScript
Programming Language*

By Brian Draper

monetary loss due to the information herein, either directly or indirectly.

Respective authors own all copyrights not held by the publisher.

The information herein is offered for informational purposes solely, and is universal as so. The presentation of the information is without contract or any type of guarantee assurance.

The trademarks that are used are without any consent, and the publication of the trademark is without permission or backing by the trademark owner. All trademarks and brands within this book are for clarifying purposes only and are the owned by the owners themselves, not affiliated with this document.

Disclaimer and Terms of Use: The Author and Publisher has strived to be as accurate and complete as possible in the creation of this book, notwithstanding the fact that he does not warrant or represent at any time that the contents within are accurate due to the rapidly changing nature of the Internet. While all attempts have been made to verify information provided in this publication, the Author and Publisher assumes no responsibility for errors, omissions, or contrary interpretation of the subject matter herein.

Any perceived slights of specific persons, peoples, or organizations are unintentional. In practical advice books, like anything else in life, there are no guarantees of results. Readers are cautioned to rely on their own judgment about their individual circumstances and act accordingly.

This book is not intended for use as a source of legal, medical, business, accounting or financial advice. All readers are advised to seek services of competent professionals in the legal, medical, business, accounting, and finance fields.

Table of Contents

Introduction to Javascript Programming

Javascript is a client-side programming language whose processing engine is embedded in web browsers like Internet Explorer, Netscape, Firefox, etc. This enables the processing engine to read and interpret web pages that contain the javascript code when browsing.

Javascript first made an appearance in 1995, although by that time it was known as Livescript. This name was later changed to javascript.

Javascript was invented to add more exciting features to HTML pages. HTML on it's on is pretty boring and it cannot do much besides display a webpage. Javascript programming, on the other hand, can provide a host of exciting features like perform calculations, allows the user to interact with webpages, perform form validations, manipulate elements on a webpage, provide excellent visual effects, enables dynamic functions and so much more.

All of this provides the user to the site with an enhanced user experience. Because javascript is a client-side language, all of these features are available in real time without the browser having to refer to the server all the time. This prevents time delays and increases user satisfaction.

JavaScript is basically a programing language created by the company Netscape. The language has gained quite a lot of popularity in the recent months as it allows the web developers to modify the browser actions as well as the contents of the site in such a manner which is not at all possible using the traditional HTML tools or even CSS. Use of JavaScript on a web page empowers the developer to control the way his page reacts, and behaves to specific actions from the user, inspect the document elements displayed on the page, validate the form options before they are submitted, check the native browser details, set cookies for specific operations, add date and time to the page, and even embed simple mini games in the website. The complete language is simple to learn and understand once you have the basic knowledge of OOPS concepts and HTML.

Software and Knowledge Needed

Before starting up with the new language, you must have a basic understanding of HTML head and body areas, and few simple statements used to add images, insert hyperlinks, make paragraphs in the hypertext language. The software which you can use for starting the JavaScript tour is basic text editor. Windows OS users may go for Notepad or Notepad++ and Mac Users can use TextEdit or TextWrangler. The code would need a web browser (preferably Mozilla Firefox or Google Chrome) for successful compilation and running.

Getting Started

A Simple Program to print a custom message in JavaScript looks something like:

```
<html>

<head>

<title>JavaScript example</title>

<script language="JavaScript">
```

\\ older Browser Versions

```
<!--

document.write("My First JavaScript Program!");

//-->

</script>

</head>

<body> Hello World! </body>

</html>
```

The use of "<!-"and "//->" in the above code ensures that the code is not displayed by older versions of browsers which lack JavaScript support. This ensures that the page does not malfunction on unsupported browsers.

Just like any other HTML file, you just need to copy paste the above code in your Notepad document, and then save it with an extension of ".html". After the save is complete, simply right click on the file, and select option "Open With". From here, choose a web browser (Mozilla Firefox if available). The code would execute on its own, and result would be displayed in the browser window.

Points to Remember

JavaScript codes are mostly placed in the "head" portion of the html but you may even use them under "body" area.

A JavaScript code normally starts with tag "<script language="JavaScript">" and ends with "</script>".

A JavaScript will always be embedded into HTML code, and it can never stand alone.

Alert Message Box

If you want to add a custom alert message box to your site, then this can be established very easily using JavaScript. The code for adding a custom alert box is as follows.

<body>

```
<script>

window.alert("This is JavaScript Alert Box!")

</script>

</body>
```

Similarly you may add other alerts like:

1. Confirm Action

Window. Confirm ("Are you sure you want to exit from this site?")

2. Prompt Action

Window.prompt("User name field cannot be left blank.")

Let's take a closer look at the great things you can do with javascript programming:

Perform Calculations

Javascript can be used to perform simple to advanced mathematical calculations. This is especially useful if you want your users to interact with your site by inputting some information that requires some sort of calculation and displaying the relevant content based on that result. For example, javascript can calculate a loan repayment and display the appropriate result if a user enters a required loan amount on the site. Furthermore, javascript can also tell date and time, time a certain activity and perform intricate date and time calculations.

User Interaction

The javascript on the webpage can take interaction from a user and perform a certain function by way events. Some of the most popular events are:

onblur

onchange

onclick

ondblclick

onfocus

onkeydown

onkeypress

onkeyup

onload

onmousedown

onmousemove

onmouseout

onmouseover

onmouseup

onselect

onsubmit

Perform Form Validations

Javascript can validate and check user input to determine whether it conforms to a certain requirement. For example, you can check if a field is left empty, if an email address is in the proper format, if a zip code code is in the proper format, etc. In most cases, if an error is made by your site visitor, an alert can display the appropriate error message to him or her.

Manipulate Elements On A Webpage

Javascript allows a user to change content or styles of a webpage upon a user interaction by way of the aforementioned events. For example, hovering over a certain text can make an image appear, text on a submit button can change on submit, etc.

Provide Visual Effects

Javascript has a host of ways to provide visual effects to a webpage that other server-side programming languages cannot. A typical example of this might be some fancy image rollover buttons.

Enables Dynamic Functions

Javascript, together with AJAX (asynchronous JavaScript and XML), can be used to create dynamic applications. One example of this is to load dynamic content onto a webpage without refreshing the page.

Can JavaScript Handle Large Scale Enterprise Applications?

According to the latest usage statistics posted on W3Techs.com, over 91% of all websites use JavaScript as a client-side programming language. There are also a number of programmers who prefer writing both client-side and server-side code in JavaScript. However, the developers have to rely on frameworks like Node.js to use JavaScript for server-side development. JavaScript can effectively handle large-scale and complex enterprise applications.

Why JavaScript can handle Complex Enterprise Applications Effectively?

Simplify Composition of Complex Enterprise Applications

The programmers can easily speedup development of a complex enterprise application by simplifying its composition. JavaScript libraries make it easier for programmers to simplify the composition of complex business applications by creating shadow DOM boundaries. The Shadow DOM make web browsers to generate and deliver documents using common HTML tags like div, select and input. In addition to decoupling the components of individual JavaScript frameworks, the shadow DOM will further facilitate seamless communication between the components. Thus, JavaScript will help programmers to maintain and manage effectively by simplifying their composition.

Responsive Web Design

Many surveys have highlighted that a large percentage of people nowadays access websites on their mobile devices. Likewise, a gradual increase is being noted in the number of organizations implementing bring your own device (BYOD) policies. So the businesses need to ensure that the enterprise application delivers quality user experience across different devices. As a modern website design technique, responsive web design helps businesses to make their web-based enterprise deliver quality user experience across a variety of devices. But responsive web design emphasizes on usage of open technologies like HTML5, JavaScript and CSS3.

Isomorphic Application Development

Many businesses nowadays opt for isomorphic JavaScript development to create web applications that deliver richer user experience across many devices. The programmers also find it easier to manage, update and maintain the isomorphic JavaScript applications. The development model requires programmers to write both client-side and server-side code in JavaScript. As the entire code base is developed using a single programming language, it becomes easier for developers to manage and update without putting any extra time and effort.

Transpilers to Simplify JavaScript Programming

JavaScript was originally designed as a client-side scripting language of web browsers. So it lacks some of the advanced features provided by modern programming languages like Java or C#. But the developers still have option to use a number of transpilers to simplify JavaScript programming. The users also have option to choose from a number of transpilers including CoffeeScript, TypeScript, DukeScript and Vaadin. These tools make it easier for programmers to add functionality to the enterprise application by making the workflow complex. These transpilers further make JavaScript effective in handling a variety of modern enterprise applications.

Availability of Many JavaScript Frameworks

Some of these JavaScript frameworks are robust and fully-featured, whereas others are simple. The programmers can use large frameworks like Angular and Ember to add functionality to the enterprise application rapidly. At the same time, they also have option to use lightweight libraries like React to accomplish a specific task efficiently. Also, they can use specialized tools like Node.js to use JavaScript as a server-side programming language. At the same time, they can avail tools like NPM to install and manage the JavaScript libraries used by the enterprise application smoothly and effectively.

On the whole, a business has option to use JavaScript for developing both frontend and backend of the enterprise applications. It can further curtail the development time and cost significantly by deploying full-stack developers to write both client-side and server-side code in JavaScript. However, the programmers will need a variety of JavaScript libraries, tools and frameworks to create more efficiently.

Four Powerful Features of JavaScript Programming Language

In the community of web developers and surfers, JavaScript is highly popular as client side scripting language for web browsers. In any web application, JavaScript can be used to implement simple features like rollover of images as well as to make asynchronous requests to server using ajax. Few years back when flash was not so popular, JavaScript was widely used to add beautiful effects to webpages and is still being used for the same purpose. Let's take a look at some of the features of this language.

1) Browser support: To access flash content, you need to install flash plugin in your browser. But to use JavaScript, you don't have to use any plugin at all. This is because all browsers have accepted JavaScript as a scripting language for them and provides integrated support for it. All you need to do is to handle some of the tasks that are dependent on DOM (Document Object Model) of different browsers properly.

2) Can be used on client side as well as on server side: As JavaScript has access to Document object model of browser, you can actually change the structure of web pages at runtime. Due to this, JavaScript can be used to add different effects to webpages. On the other hand, JavaScript could be

used on the server side as well. For example, in Alfresco which is a popular open source enterprise content management system, JavaScript is used in creating webscripts. This makes adding custom tasks to alfresco quite simple.

3) Functional programming language: In JavaScript, function could be assigned to variables just like any other data types. Not only that, but a function can accept another function as a parameter and can also return a function. You can have functions with no name as well. Clearly, this gives you the ability to code in functional programming style.

4) Support for objects: JavaScript is an object oriented language. However, the way JavaScript handles objects and inheritance is bit different from conventional object oriented programming languages like Java. Due to this, JavaScript supports most of the object oriented concepts while being simple to learn and use.

These are some of the features that give JavaScript an ability to handle simple as well as complex tasks. Due to this, JavaScript has remained as the most popular programming language for a long time. It is also a good language for people who want to learn computer programming as it supports object oriented as well as function concepts and to use it, you just need a browser and a text editor.

How to Get Rid of the JavaScript Warning on Internet Explorer

JavaScript is the standard programming language for web pages on the internet. JavaScript errors are bugs in the programming code for a page.

Back at the dawn of the internet, web pages were limited to using the Hypertext Markup Language (HTML). HTML is a standard used by all browsers to display web pages. HTML handles things like font styles, links, and pictures, which was enough at first, but people wanted to do more with web pages.

Netscape used a simple programming language developed for JavaScript so that even non-programmers could enhance their websites with functionality that is more sophisticated. The language itself has become more sophisticated and is now a standard which, like HTML, is supported by all web browsers.

JavaScript was not designed to run extremely complex programs; it was designed for simple enhancements to web pages. As the internet has evolved, the programming behind web pages has become more complex, often straining the limits of JavaScript. To alleviate the problem some of the programming has been offloaded to servers rather than trying to download it all onto your computer.

JavaScript, which runs locally, is currently used heavily by websites to drive their user interfaces. Although many modern websites communicate with servers to get their data, that communication can be slow or even fail altogether. It is important for the user interface to be responsive even if there is a problem with the server, so the interface is usually written in JavaScript and run locally from your computer, while the more complex code runs on a server.

As with any programming language, JavaScript will have bugs in it, and sometimes they will cause the program to fail. Fortunately, unlike a desktop program, when a JavaScript program fails, the rest of the page usually still works fine.

Getting Rid of the JavaScript Warning Dialog on Internet Explorer

Most JavaScript errors you get are due to a failure in a single webpage. Usually these errors are harmless: Although you may lose some functionality, they are not a danger to your computer.

However, Internet Explorer pops up a warning dialog by default. This warning stops you from doing anything on the page and can be annoying. If you are a programmer it may be interesting to look at the code, but for the rest of us it is not very useful.

To get rid of the dialog, follow these steps:

1. In Internet Explorer, select Internet Options from the Tools menu.
2. Click on the Advanced tab.
3. Depending on your version there may be up to three checkboxes you need to set (two of them checked, one unchecked):

o Check: Disable script debugging (Internet Explorer)
o Check: Disable script debugging (Other)
o Uncheck: Display a notification about every script error

4. Click the OK button.

This should stop the warning dialog from showing. If you start having problems with many web pages, there may be a problem with your browser, not with the web page, and you may need to reinstall Internet Explorer.

Errors About JavaScript

For most computer users javascript is strange PC lingo. Most people except PC professionals programmers know little about it. Essentially, JavaScript is a web development language that is most commonly used on websites. Popular among non-programmers for its user-friendly nature, JavaScript also allows scripting access to objects embedded in other applications.

However, JavaScript errors are fairly common too, largely because so many amateurs write web development programs using it. But the terrible thing is that it can also be used to write adware and spyware, which make their way into your computer, often without you realizing it, and thereby clog the registry. This in turn slows down your computer and may even cause it to crash, and we all know what a big headache that means.

The common JavaScript errors are following:
1. JavaScript is not enabled in the browser.
2. The web page contains a JavaScript programming error.
3. The browser does not support JavaScript technology.

What can we do to deal with these problems? Of course, you could choose to inform the Webmaster about the problem and supply all details of the javascript error message that you have been receiving, but you have an easier alternative to that. Simply clean your windows registry and watch the problem vanish.

For those not in the know, the windows registry is a vast internal database in which all programs that you use on your system, including windows itself, store a huge volume of data. So whenever you make a change to the Control Panel settings, file associations, system policies, or install new software, the changes reflect in the registry. So the registry actually monitors the way your system behaves, and unless you keep windows registry clean by using Registry Cleaner tool regularly, you will not get away from JavaScript error messages.

Easy Tips You Can Use to Remove a JavaScript Error

Many website builders rely on JavaScript to make their websites functional. Functions such as drop down menus, image changes, and linking to other websites are all done through the JavaScript program. When a JavaScript error pops up, that means that there is something incorrect in the coding.

Letting JavaScript Errors Run on Your Website Could Cost Money

Experiencing a JavaScript error can be devastating for some website builders. It is a common error, but even a simple error can ruin the outcome of the website and make it confusing and frustrating for the end users. This can, in turn, cost the builder money as well as lose business.

Disable Error Alerts for the Firefox Browser

One way to help break the constant cycle of pop up error alerts is to manually change the option to enable or disable alert message pop ups. To disable these alerts for the Mozilla Firefox user do the following:

1. Select the "Tool" tab at the top of the page

2. Click "Options" and select the "Content" tab at the top of the box

3. Disable the alerts by unchecking the box "Enable JavaScript"

This will disable the alerts from interrupting you on the internet. However, even though the alerts are disabled, it does not mean that the errors are gone for good.

Try Using a Different Web Browser

Different web browsers react differently to different websites. Where one browser might encounter an error, the other will not. If the errors still occur through other browsers, try using someone else's account and even someone else's computer. If the errors stop when using someone else's PC, then it may be time to focus on cleaning your PC's registry.

Remove Temporary Internet Files from Internet Explorer

Your internet browser makes copies of the places you go and stores them in temporary files. A build up of these files can create errors in the system and they need to be emptied periodically. For Internet Explorer users do the following:

1. Select the "Tools" tab located at the top of the page
2. Select the "General" tab
3. Under "Temporary Internet Files" select "Settings"
4. Click "Delete Files" and hit "OK"
5. Click "Delete Cookies" and hit "OK"
6. Also, under "History" select "Clear History"
7. Select "Yes" and then click "OK"

Maintain Your PC's Registry

Fix the JavaScript error if it still persists with a registry cleaner. Constant use of a PC can wear it down and the constant flow of information can clog up your registry, slowing down your computer. These errors can result from a faulty or corrupt registry.

Optimize-Your-PC can provide you with advanced registry cleaning technology. It will scan, diagnose, and repair your JavaScript Error, leaving you with nothing but a highly-optimized PC.

Adding JavaScript in Dreamweaver 8

JavaScript allows you to add interactive elements to and perform scripted functions on Web pages. Adding JavaScript in Dreamweaver 8 is not difficult, and does not require you to know JavaScript programming.

In Dreamweaver 8, JavaScript is a "behavior" and is controlled through the Behaviours panel. You'll use the Behaviours panel when adding JavaScript in Dreamweaver 8 to a Web page you're working with.

To open the Behaviours panel, select Windows > Behaviours. Select the + button to activate a drop-down menu. The Add Behaviours drop down menu contains about two-dozen common JavaScript-controlled functions you may add to a page in Dreamweaver. Common functions like checking browser types and revisions, checking for a plug-in, displaying a Pop-up message, validating a form or going to a URL are examples of JavaScript behaviours you may add.

Each behaviour in the Add Behaviours menu has a dialogue box that enables you to specify the actions that should take place when a certain trigger is encountered. A trigger is an action that a visitor to your Web site may perform, such as clicking on a link, entering data into a form or mousing over a particular location on the page.

You'll find the Validate Form behaviour useful if you collect typed information from your visitors. The Validate Form behaviour can used to verify that data entered by a visitor is in the correct format or contains only valid data. Once you have configured the behaviour appropriately, select OK.

If the behaviour you want to add is not among the built-in JavaScript behaviours, you may select Get More Behaviours. This selection will take you to the Macromedia Dreamweaver Exchange Site. Here you'll find user-created JavaScript behaviours that you may download. One caution: not all behaviours at this location are free of charge, but you'll find that adding new behaviours to your Dreamweaver interface is easy when you visit this site.

You may also change a behaviour you have added to Dreamweaver 8. To modify an existing behaviour, find the behaviour you want to edit in Code View. Select it and it will appear in the list below the Add Behaviours button in the Behaviours panel. From this point, you may modify the order in which events occur, change the event that triggers an action or delete the behaviour altogether.

How Good Is JavaScript for Building a Large Scale Web Application?

According to the most recent statistics posted on w3techs.com, more than 89% of websites currently use JavaScript as a client-side programming language. As a cross-platform and lightweight programming language, JavaScript makes it easier for programmers to build responsive websites and web applications that work with seamlessly with popular web browsers, operating systems and devices. It is also widely used by programmers as part of the web browsers to accomplish important tasks like browser control, user interaction, and asynchronous communication.

Also, the programmers have option to use JavaScript as a server-side scripting language through Node.js and similar runtime environment. At the same time, they also can use a variety of open source frameworks to reduce the amount of time and effort required for building JavaScript applications. It can also be used along with HTML5 and CSS for creating web applications and games. So you can always consider using JavaScript as a dynamic client-side programming language for building large scale web applications.

Advantages of Using JavaScript for Large Scale Web Application Development

Supported by Major Web Browsers

JavaScript is supported by most of the widely used web browsers including Firefox, Chrome, Internet Explorer, Safari and Opera. It is also supported by the new web browsers whose vendors have implemented JavaScript. So the users can access the web applications using JavaScript regardless of their choice of web browser. They also have option to access all functionality of the website by enabling the scripting language if it is disable due to some reason.

No Need to Use Any Specific Tools

JavaScript is an interpreted programming language. So you can easily write the code without using any specific tool or program. You can simply open a notepad, and start writing JavaScript code. Also, you have option to use a number of editors to identify the mistakes in the code. The editors colorize or reformat the script to make it easier for users to identify the errors.

Option to Reuse the Code

You can further reuse the JavaScript code across multiple pages simply by placing the code in separate files. After placing the code in a separate file, you have to save the file with.js extension. The file can be linked to multiple web pages by using the <script> tag to the HTML code of the page. The option enables you to avoid writing additional code while adding the same functionality to various parts of the website.

Many Libraries and Frameworks

You have option to reduce the time and effort required for building large JavaScript applications by using several frameworks and libraries. Many programmers prefer using dynamic JavaScript frameworks like AngularJS, Backbone, Ember and React. However, you still have option to choose from a long list of JavaScript libraries according to your specific needs. For instance, you can effectuate GUI development using widgets like DHTMLX, Bootstrap, jQuery UI, DojoWidgets or AngularJS. Likewise, you use popular template systems like jQuery Mobile, Handlebars, Mustache and Cascade Framework.

Comparatively Faster

As noted earlier, JavaScript is a client-side scripting language. So the code is executed on user's system. As the code is executed without any server interaction, the processing is done at a comparatively faster. The faster processing enables the web application to keep the users engaged by delivering richer browsing experience.

Deliver Updated Response Data from the Server

JavaScript further uses the XmlHttpRequest API for data retrieval. The API sends HTTP or HTTPS requests to the web server, and load the response sent by the server in the script. The script can easily update the current web page based on the response data received from the server without reloading a new web page. So you can boost the web application's performance by providing updated information to the users without reloading the web page completely.

Extend the Website's Functionality

JavaScript makes it easier for you to extend the functionality of the web application without putting any extra effort. You can use the scripting language to create visual effects on the screen, calculate data, and make web pages more interactive. JavaScript further allows you to extend the website's functionality by using third-party scripts. The flexibility makes it easier for you to add out-of-box features to the web application without using any additional plug-ins or tools.

Reduces Load on Server

The server-side scripting languages require the web server to process the user request before response is sent to the user. So the process required additional time despite the user having a high-speed internet connection. But the JavaScript code is processed on the user's machine, without interacting with the web browser. Thus, the strain and load on the web server is reduced drastically, while the user gets quick response. You can use JavaScript while building large scale websites to provide faster response to users without putting excess strain on the server.

Optimizes Local Caching

JavaScript can be used along with HTML5 to enable users to access websites even when there is not active internet connection. The technologies are effective in caching data locally, and keep the web application responsive till the internet connection is restored. You can even use tools like Kendo UI DataSource to track changes made to an object locally, and upload the changes to the web server once the network connection is restored. The option enables you to make the web applications work just like mobile apps.

Works with Other Web Technologies

As mentioned earlier, JavaScript developers can be used as both client side and server side scripting language. At the same time, you also have option to use JavaScript as a client side technology along with some of the widely used web technologies like PHP, Perl and Java. The scripting language is also used widely along with HTML5 and CSS for developing responsive websites accessible on a variety of devices using the same code base.

However, you must keep in mind some of the major shortcomings of JavaScript while using it for building large websites and web applications. As JavaScript code is executed on the web browser, it becomes vulnerable to various security attacks. Also, the code becomes unpredictable as individual browsers interpret it differently.

Major bots of major search engines including Google cannot understand the client-side code written in JavaScript completely and fully. So the search engine ranking and visibility of the web applications using too much JavaScript will be impacted. But you can still use JavaScript along with other popular web technologies like HTML5 and CSS to create robust web applications accessible on multiple devices, operating systems and web browsers.

Why Would Companies Hire JavaScript Developers?

Companies are of late putting more emphasis on hiring JavaScript developers. The businesses are nowadays spending a good deal of money, time as well as efforts to recruit talented, especially the younger and fresher ones mainly for their quality of expertise and because of the fact that they are in tune with the latest technology and trend of development.

Now, there are a number of reasons why modern businesses are putting their money on JavaScript developers.

The primary reason why businesses bank on these is their background education. Most of candidates have a bachelor's degree in software engineering, computer science, information technology and other degrees that are pertinent with the niche of business that is run by the companies.

However, certain businesses put more emphasis on the experienced, rather than the degrees they possess. That is a different issue altogether though.

Businesses put money because of a solid understanding of the software development life cycle which these professionals have. Plus, they have a strong concept - a fact that augments their programming skills for the client-side as well as server-side languages. This is extremely important as not every project or client needs only JavaScript but the ancillary programming platforms as well. Moreover, when it comes to personal traits, these professionals have extremely strong analytical skills along with trouble shooting expertise - a fact that comes in extremely handy in software development. Moreover, they have the needed psychological getup to work in sync with others in a team. That is itself a reason enough for companies to hire them.

Apart from all these issues, good to know their responsibilities and have an excellent professional outlook that make all the difference. The majority of the JavaScript development programs are particularly designed as well as developed for web-based along with different server-based applications that are generally used on web sites and computer systems.

After development, it is necessary to evaluate the programs properly. A good developer would also have the expertise to evaluate these programming scripts and hence, companies hire them to cut costs as a programmer will be able to develop as well as evaluate the scripts. They are also expert in testing the language extensively to see whether it is functioning properly before it is handed over to the client. They also ensure that the script is totally free of bugs.

These professionals, especially the fresh pass outs have an extensive knowledge on the latest Java Virtual Machine or JVM languages and this helps them complete the tasks faster. They are also are expert in building an application that will make the language simpler. This at the end of the day saves a lot of money for the companies.

The key for the companies is to look for the best engineers who are involved in the software development community so that they are in tune with the latest technology and are fresh from the point of view of concept-creation. This is to make sure that the businesses get maximum return from the investment they put on JavaScript developers who are the mainstay of business development.

Experts are not only skilled and experienced, but they are proficient in other languages as well, like c, C++, Net, Python, Joomla and so on. They have impeccable skills. So, though hiring such a professional is quite cost-effective, taking into account today's inflation, still companies vie on them as this pays off in the short as well as long run subsequently. However, in order to save costs of late companies are growing a propensity of hiring offshore professionals instead of employing individuals on a full time basis. These professionals offer maintenance as well as other ancillary services at no additional costs and this helps the companies to cut costs to a large extent.

JavaScript Where To

The <script> Tag

In HTML, JavaScript code must be inserted between <script> and </script> tags.

Example

```
<script>
document.getElementById("demo").innerHTML    =    "My First JavaScript";
</script>
```

Old JavaScript examples may use a type attribute: <script type="text/javascript">.
The type attribute is not required. JavaScript is the default scripting language in HTML.

JavaScript in <head> or <body>
You can place any number of scripts in an HTML document.

Scripts can be placed in the <body>, or in the <head> section of an HTML page, or in both.

JavaScript in <head>

In this example, a JavaScript function is placed in the <head> section of an HTML page.

The function is invoked (called) when a button is clicked:

Example
```
<!DOCTYPE html>
<html>
<head>
<script>
function myFunction() {
   document.getElementById("demo").innerHTML         =
"Paragraph changed.";
}
</script>
</head>

<body>

<h1>A Web Page</h1>
<p id="demo">A Paragraph</p>
<button      type="button"      onclick="myFunction()">Try
it</button>

</body>
</html>
```

JavaScript in <body>

In this example, a JavaScript function is placed in the <body> section of an HTML page.

The function is invoked (called) when a button is clicked:

Example
```
<!DOCTYPE html>
<html>
<body>

<h1>A Web Page</h1>
<p id="demo">A Paragraph</p>
<button type="button" onclick="myFunction()">Try it</button>

<script>
function myFunction() {
  document.getElementById("demo").innerHTML = "Paragraph changed.";
}
</script>

</body>
</html>
```

External JavaScript

External file: myScript.js

```
function myFunction() {
  document.getElementById("demo").innerHTML   =
  "Paragraph changed.";
}
```

External scripts are practical when the same code is used in many different web pages.

JavaScript files have the file extension .js.

To use an external script, put the name of the script file in the src (source) attribute of a <script> tag:

Example
```
<!DOCTYPE html>
<html>
<body>

<script src="myScript.js"></script>

</body>
</html>
```

You can place an external script reference in <head> or <body> as you like.

The script will behave as if it was located exactly where the <script> tag is located.
External scripts cannot contain <script> tags.

External JavaScript Advantages
Placing scripts in external files has some advantages:

It separates HTML and code
It makes HTML and JavaScript easier to read and maintain
Cached JavaScript files can speed up page loads
To add several script files to one page - use several script tags:

Example
```
<script src="myScript1.js"></script>
<script src="myScript2.js"></script>
```
External References

External scripts can be referenced with a full URL or with a path relative to the current web page.

This example uses a full URL to link to a script:

Example
```
<script
src="http://www.w3schools.com/js/myScript1.js"></script>
```

This example links to a script located in the same folder as the current page:

Example
```
<script src="myScript1.js"></script>
```

JavaScript Output

JavaScript Display Possibilities
JavaScript can "display" data in different ways:

Writing into an alert box, using window.alert().
Writing into the HTML output using document.write().
Writing into an HTML element, using innerHTML.
Writing into the browser console, using console.log().
Using window.alert()
You can use an alert box to display data:

Example
```
<!DOCTYPE html>
<html>
<body>

<h1>My First Web Page</h1>
<p>My first paragraph.</p>

<script>
window.alert(5 + 6);
</script>

</body>
</html>
```

Using document.write()

For testing purposes, it is convenient to use document.write():

Example
```
<!DOCTYPE html>
<html>
<body>

<h1>My First Web Page</h1>
<p>My first paragraph.</p>

<script>
document.write(5 + 6);
</script>

</body>
</html>
```

Using document.write() after an HTML document is fully loaded, will delete all existing HTML:

Example

```
<!DOCTYPE html>
<html>
<body>

<h1>My First Web Page</h1>
<p>My first paragraph.</p>

<button onclick="document.write(5 + 6)">Try it</button>

</body>
</html>
```

Using innerHTML

To access an HTML element, JavaScript can use the document.getElementById(id) method.

The id attribute defines the HTML element. The innerHTML property defines the HTML content:

Example

```
<!DOCTYPE html>
<html>
<body>

<h1>My First Web Page</h1>
<p>My First Paragraph</p>

<p id="demo"></p>

<script>
document.getElementById("demo").innerHTML = 5 + 6;
</script>

</body>
</html>
```

To "display data" in HTML, (in most cases) you will set the value of an innerHTML property.

Using console.log()

In your browser, you can use the console.log() method to display data.

Example

```
<!DOCTYPE html>
<html>
<body>

<h1>My First Web Page</h1>
<p>My first paragraph.</p>

<script>
console.log(5 + 6);
</script>

</body>
</html>
```

JavaScript Syntax

JavaScript syntax is the set of rules, how JavaScript programs are constructed.

JavaScript Programs

A computer program is a list of "instructions" to be "executed" by the computer.

In a programming language, these program instructions are called statements.

JavaScript is a programming language.

JavaScript statements are separated by semicolons:

Example
```
var x, y, z;
x = 5;
y = 6;
z = x + y;
```

In HTML, JavaScript programs are executed by the web browser.

JavaScript Statements
JavaScript statements are composed of:

Values, Operators, Expressions, Keywords, and Comments.

JavaScript Values

The JavaScript syntax defines two types of values: Fixed values and variable values.

Fixed values are called literals. Variable values are called variables.

JavaScript Literals

The most important rules for writing fixed values are:

Numbers are written with or without decimals:

10.50

1001

Strings are text, written within double or single quotes:

"John Doe"

'John Doe'

JavaScript Variables

In a programming language, variables are used to store data values.

JavaScript uses the var keyword to declare variables.

An equal sign is used to assign values to variables.

In this example, x is defined as a variable. Then, x is assigned (given) the value 6:

```
var x;
```

```
x = 6;
```

JavaScript Operators

JavaScript uses an assignment operator (=) to assign values to variables:

var x, y;
x = 5;
y = 6;
JavaScript uses arithmetic operators (+ - * /) to compute values:

JavaScript Expressions

An expression is a combination of values, variables, and operators, which computes to a value.

The computation is called an evaluation.

For example, 5 * 10 evaluates to 50:

5 * 10

Expressions can also contain variable values:

x * 10

The values can be of various types, such as numbers and strings.

For example, "John" + " " + "Doe", evaluates to "John Doe":

"John" + " " + "Doe"

JavaScript Keywords

JavaScript keywords are used to identify actions to be performed.

The var keyword tells the browser to create variables:

```
var x, y;
x = 5 + 6;
y = x * 10;
```

JavaScript Comments
Not all JavaScript statements are "executed".

Code after double slashes // or between /* and */ is treated as a comment.

Comments are ignored, and will not be executed:

var x = 5; // I will be executed

// var x = 6; I will NOT be executed

Try it Yourself »
You will learn more about comments in a later chapter.

JavaScript Identifiers

Identifiers are names.

In JavaScript, identifiers are used to name variables (and keywords, and functions, and labels).

The rules for legal names are much the same in most programming languages.

In JavaScript, the first character must be a letter, an underscore (_), or a dollar sign ($).

Subsequent characters may be letters, digits, underscores, or dollar signs.

Numbers are not allowed as the first character.
This way JavaScript can easily distinguish identifiers from numbers.

JavaScript is Case Sensitive
All JavaScript identifiers are case sensitive.

The variables lastName and lastname, are two different variables.

```
var lastname, lastName;
lastName = "Doe";
lastname = "Peterson";
```

JavaScript does not interpret VAR or Var as the keyword var.

JavaScript and Camel Case

Historically, programmers have used three ways of joining multiple words into one variable name:

Hyphens:

first-name, last-name, master-card, inter-city.

Hyphens are not allowed in JavaScript. It is reserved for subtractions.

Underscore:

first_name, last_name, master_card, inter_city.

Camel Case:

FirstName, LastName, MasterCard, InterCity.

camelCase

JavaScript programmers tend to use camel case that starts with a lowercase letter:

firstName, lastName, masterCard, interCity.

JavaScript Character Set

JavaScript uses the Unicode character set.

Unicode covers (almost) all the characters, punctuations, and symbols in the world.

JavaScript Statements

This statement tells the browser to write "Hello Dolly." inside an HTML element with id="demo":

Example

document.getElementById("demo").innerHTML = "Hello Dolly.";

JavaScript Programs
Most JavaScript programs contain many JavaScript statements.

The statements are executed, one by one, in the same order as they are written.

In this example x, y, and z are given values, and finally z is displayed:

Example
```
var x, y, z;
x = 5;
y = 6;
z = x + y;
document.getElementById("demo").innerHTML = z;
```

JavaScript programs (and JavaScript statements) are often called JavaScript code.

Semicolons ;

Semicolons separate JavaScript statements.

Add a semicolon at the end of each executable statement:

```
var a, b, c;
a = 5;
b = 6;
c = a + b;
```

When separated by semicolons, multiple statements on one line are allowed:

```
a = 5; b = 6; c = a + b;
```

On the web, you might see examples without semicolons.

Ending statements with semicolon is not required, but highly recommended.

JavaScript White Space

JavaScript ignores multiple spaces. You can add white space to your script to make it more readable.

The following lines are equivalent:

```
var person = "Hege";
var person="Hege";
```

A good practice is to put spaces around operators (= + - * /):

```
var x = y + z;
```

JavaScript Line Length and Line Breaks

For best readability, programmers often like to avoid code lines longer than 80 characters.

If a JavaScript statement does not fit on one line, the best place to break it, is after an operator:

Example
document.getElementById("demo").innerHTML =
"Hello Dolly.";

JavaScript Code Blocks

JavaScript statements can be grouped together in code blocks, inside curly brackets {...}.

The purpose of code blocks is to define statements to be executed together.

One place you will find statements grouped together in blocks, is in JavaScript functions:

Example

```
function myFunction() {
    document.getElementById("demo1").innerHTML    =
"Hello Dolly.";
    document.getElementById("demo2").innerHTML    =
"How are you?";
}
```

JavaScript Keywords

JavaScript statements often start with a keyword to identify the JavaScript action to be performed.

Here is a list of some of the keywords you will learn about in this tutorial:

Keyword	Description
break	- Terminates a switch or a loop
continue	- Jumps out of a loop and starts at the top
debugger	- Stops the execution of JavaScript, and calls (if available) the debugging function
do ... while	Executes a block of statements, and repeats the block, while a condition is true
for	Marks a block of statements to be executed, as long as a condition is true
function	Declares a function

if ... else   Marks a block of statements to be executed, depending on a condition

return   Exits a function

switch   Marks a block of statements to be executed, depending on different cases

try ... catch Implements error handling to a block of statements

var   Declares a variable

JavaScript Comments

JavaScript comments can be used to explain JavaScript code, and to make it more readable.

JavaScript comments can also be used to prevent execution, when testing alternative code.

Single Line Comments
Single line comments start with //.

Any text between // and the end of the line will be ignored by JavaScript (will not be executed).

This example uses a single-line comment before each code line:

Example

```
// Change heading:
document.getElementById("myH").innerHTML = "My First Page";
// Change paragraph:
document.getElementById("myP").innerHTML = "My first paragraph.";
```

This example uses a single line comment at the end of each line to explain the code:

Example
var x = 5;   // Declare x, give it the value of 5
var y = x + 2; // Declare y, give it the value of x + 2

Multi-line Comments
Multi-line comments start with /* and end with */.

Any text between /* and */ will be ignored by JavaScript.

This example uses a multi-line comment (a comment block) to explain the code:

Example
/*
The code below will change
the heading with id = "myH"
and the paragraph with id = "myP"
in my web page:
*/
document.getElementById("myH").innerHTML = "My First Page";
document.getElementById("myP").innerHTML = "My first paragraph.";

Using Comments to Prevent Execution

Using comments to prevent execution of code is suitable for code testing.

Adding // in front of a code line changes the code lines from an executable line to a comment.

This example uses // to prevent execution of one of the code lines:

Example
```
//document.getElementById("myH").innerHTML   =   "My
First Page";
document.getElementById("myP").innerHTML = "My first
paragraph.";
```

This example uses a comment block to prevent execution of multiple lines:

Example
```
/*
document.getElementById("myH").innerHTML = "My First
Page";
document.getElementById("myP").innerHTML = "My first
paragraph.";
*/
```

JavaScript Variables

JavaScript Variables

JavaScript variables are containers for storing data values.

In this example, x, y, and z, are variables:

Example
var x = 5;
var y = 6;
var z = x + y;

From the example above, you can expect:

* x stores the value 5
* y stores the value 6
* z stores the value 11

Much Like Algebra
In this example, price1, price2, and total, are variables:

Example
```
var price1 = 5;
var price2 = 6;
var total = price1 + price2;
```

In programming, just like in algebra, we use variables (like price1) to hold values.

In programming, just like in algebra, we use variables in expressions (total = price1 + price2).

From the example above, you can calculate the total to be 11.

JavaScript variables are containers for storing data values.

JavaScript Identifiers

All JavaScript variables must be identified with unique names.

These unique names are called identifiers.

Identifiers can be short names (like x and y) or more descriptive names (age, sum, totalVolume).

The general rules for constructing names for variables (unique identifiers) are:

* Names can contain letters, digits, underscores, and dollar signs.
* Names must begin with a letter
* Names can also begin with $ and _ (but we will not use it in this tutorial)
* Names are case sensitive (y and Y are different variables)
* Reserved words (like JavaScript keywords) cannot be used as names

JavaScript identifiers are case-sensitive.

The Assignment Operator
In JavaScript, the equal sign (=) is an "assignment" operator, not an "equal to" operator.

This is different from algebra. The following does not make sense in algebra:

x = x + 5
In JavaScript, however, it makes perfect sense: it assigns the value of x + 5 to x.

(It calculates the value of x + 5 and puts the result into x. The value of x is incremented by 5.)

The "equal to" operator is written like == in JavaScript.

JavaScript Data Types
JavaScript variables can hold numbers like 100 and text values like "John Doe".

In programming, text values are called text strings.

JavaScript can handle many types of data, but for now, just think of numbers and strings.

Strings are written inside double or single quotes. Numbers are written without quotes.

If you put a number in quotes, it will be treated as a text string.

Example

```
var pi = 3.14;
var person = "John Doe";
var answer = 'Yes I am!';
```

Declaring (Creating) JavaScript Variables

Creating a variable in JavaScript is called "declaring" a variable.

You declare a JavaScript variable with the var keyword:

var carName;
After the declaration, the variable has no value. (Technically it has the value of undefined)

To assign a value to the variable, use the equal sign:

carName = "Volvo";
You can also assign a value to the variable when you declare it:

var carName = "Volvo";
In the example below, we create a variable called carName and assign the value "Volvo" to it.

Then we "output" the value inside an HTML paragraph with id="demo":

Example
```
<p id="demo"></p>

<script>
var carName = "Volvo";
document.getElementById("demo").innerHTML        =
carName;
</script>
```

One Statement, Many Variables
You can declare many variables in one statement.

Start the statement with var and separate the variables by comma:

```
var person = "John Doe", carName = "Volvo", price = 200;
```

A declaration can span multiple lines:

var person = "John Doe",
carName = "Volvo",
price = 200;

Value = undefined

In computer programs, variables are often declared without a value. The value can be something that has to be calculated, or something that will be provided later, like user input.

A variable declared without a value will have the value undefined.

The variable carName will have the value undefined after the execution of this statement:

Example
var carName;

Re-Declaring JavaScript Variables
If you re-declare a JavaScript variable, it will not lose its value.

The variable carName will still have the value "Volvo" after the execution of these statements:

Example
var carName = "Volvo";
var carName;
JavaScript Arithmetic
As with algebra, you can do arithmetic with JavaScript variables, using operators like = and +:

Example
var x = 5 + 2 + 3;

You can also add strings, but strings will be concatenated:

Example
var x = "John" + " " + "Doe";

Also try this:

Example
var x = "5" + 2 + 3;

JavaScript Operators

Example
Assign values to variables and add them together:

```
var x = 5;       // assign the value 5 to x
var y = 2;       // assign the value 2 to y
var z = x + y;   // assign the value 7 to z (x + y)
```

The assignment operator (=) assigns a value to a variable.

Assignment
```
var x = 10;
```

Adding
```
var x = 5;
var y = 2;
var z = x + y;
```

The multiplication operator (*) multiplies numbers.

Multiplying
```
var x = 5;
var y = 2;
var z = x * y;
```

JavaScript Arithmetic Operators

Arithmetic operators are used to perform arithmetic on numbers:

Operator Description
+ Addition
- Subtraction
* Multiplication
/ Division
% Modulus
++ Increment
-- Decrement

The addition assignment operator (+=) adds a value to a variable.

Assignment
var x = 10;
x += 5;
Assignment operators are fully described in the JS Assignment chapter.

JavaScript String Operators

The + operator can also be used to add (concatenate) strings.

Example

The += assignment operator can also be used to add (concatenate) strings:

Example
txt1 = "What a very ";
txt1 += "nice day";
The result of txt1 will be:

What a very nice day

When used on strings, the + operator is called the concatenation operator.

Adding Strings and Numbers

Adding two numbers, will return the sum, but adding a number and a string will return a string:

Example

```
x = 5 + 5;
y = "5" + 5;
z = "Hello" + 5;
```

The result of x, y, and z will be:

10
55
Hello5

If you add a number and a string, the result will be a string!

JavaScript Comparison Operators

Operator Description

== equal to

=== equal value and equal type

!= not equal

!== not equal value or not equal type

> greater than

< less than

>= greater than or equal to

<= less than or equal to

? ternary operator

JavaScript   Logical Operators
Operator   Description
&&   logical and
|| logical or
!   logical not

JavaScript   Type Operators
Operator   Description
typeof   Returns the type of a variable
instanceof   Returns true if an object is an instance of an
object type

Java and JavaScript: Not the Same

A common problem for programmers is confusing the two programming languages Java and JavaScript. While the two languages share
some similarities, they are very different beasts and generally used in different applications.

Java is a general-purpose programming language developed by Sun Microsystems as a way to let programmers "write-once, run
anywhere". Java code is executed inside a virtual machine, so a Java application can be distributed without the developer having to
worry about the different architectures and operating systems that the application might run on.

JavaScript, on the other hand, is a scripting language. It's only purpose is inside of web pages. When a web browser loads the page, it
executes the JavaScript code inside it. The code can change how the web page looks and operates. For example, JavaScript code can be
used to create a drop down menu that expands when you mouse over it, or an image gallery where the displayed image changes every so
often.

This difference is most obvious in the libraries of the two languages. Java has a large standard library that's been standardized in the

Java standard. This allows Java programmers to use a wide variety of tools when writing code. JavaScript's standard library is much

smaller and generally related to working with the HTML code in the web page.

Further confusing the two languages is the fact that Java can also be used in a web page in the form of a Java applet. This is a small

part of the web page where Java code runs and is displayed in the browser window. Java applets are generally used to create more

advanced things in the browser, a game for example. JavaScript is not nearly powerful enough to create a complex game, so Java is used.

This is where Java's platform-independent advantage comes in. As long as the web browser has the Java plugin (and most do), the code

will run the same no matter which web browser is used. This cannot be said for JavaScript, which is often implemented differently in the

different web browsers, requiring various compatibility hacks.

And despite the fact that both can be used as web languages, JavaScript is vastly more important for the aspiring web programmer to

learn. JavaScript's simplicity also means that it runs quickly, so that small things you may want to add to a web page aren't bogged down

by Java's virtual machine. This is a reason why Java isn't used much on the web anymore: because it's slow. A Java applet requires

loading the large Java plugin and is overkill for all but large web projects, especially when more flexible tools such as HTML5 are

becoming more widely used on the web.

Java and JavaScript are two different programming languages. Each of them have their uses,but they are not interchangeable with each

other.

How to Use JavaScript to Get User Entry and Use the Entry in a Calculation

The use of variables are key to all programming languages. You may remember the x's and y's from your high school algebra class. In programming, variables have even more meaning than just some vague idea of an unknown value. In programming, a variable is used as the name of a particular information storage area. You can then use that variable name to call whatever you happened to store there. If you throw away the old stuff and put something new in the storage are, the variable calls the new stuff.

Some programming languages have to know ahead of time what you plan to store. They like to plan ahead of time what size storage area you are renting. Telling these language what you plan to store means that you have to declare a data type. These types of programming languages are called strongly typed languages. Other languages, such as JavaScript, could care less what kind of stuff you are storing.

They decide what size space you need when you send it to the storage area. That is one reason JavaScript is less complicated to learn than some programming languages.

However, there are still some things you will need to learn about data types because there are some side effects to not telling what type of information you want to store.

In any case, the information still has a variable name. Here is an exercise that

1) gathers information from a prompt box,
2) puts it into a variable,
3) does a calculation, and
4) sends the answer back in an alert.

Add this code to the of a new web page

```
var SquareThis = prompt("Enter a number you would like to square.");
var Answer;

Answer = SquareThis * SquareThis;

alert(Answer);
```

Basic Programming Skills in this Bit of Code

1. When you do any kind of programming, you have to think of what pieces of information the computer will need to identify and hold on
to. Then you make variables to hold the information. In this example, we need to hold two pieces of information, 1) the number that will
be squared, 2) the answer.

2. You tell JavaScript that you want it to store information by naming var, a space and a variable name.

3. The first line of this script does three jobs, 1) it tells JavaScript to set aside memory space for the variable SquareThis, 2) it uses a pre- written function to prompt the user for a number, 3) it takes whatever the user types in the prompt box and puts it in the memory space for SquareThis.

4. Notice that the function prompt requires an argument just like the alert() did. Notice too that the argument is in " ", which means that the argument is a String data type.

5. Now the script needs a variable to hold the answer. This is done with "var Answer;"
6. Everything is in place now to do the math: "Answer = SquareThis * SquareThis;" The part that tells the computer what kind of math to do is called an operator. The main operators are +, -, *, / (add, subtract, multiply, divide). There

are many other operators, as well. A square is any number multiplied by itself; so this formula multiplies SquareThis by SquareThis.

7. The program has an answer, but it needs to tell the user. Again, we will use an alert box.

8. Now change the formula to do something else. Try adding another variable and another alert() to ask for another number (or several.)

Here are some operators for you to experiment with:

Operator

JavaScript Math Functions

+ Adds two numbers

- Subtracts two numbers

/ Divides two numbers

++ Adds one to a number (only needs one variable)

-- Subracts one from a number (only needs one variable)

Conclusion

HTML may not be used instead of JavaScript. Both these programming languages are completely different and have different functions,
features and capabilities. While HTML is a markup language and is designed to create static web page content, JavaScript is a programming language that can perform dynamic tasks. It can be used again and again on different pages of a site. This can be done by externalizing and placing it in separate files and linking a JavaScript file to the HTML code of the particular page. Hence, JavaScript can be added to many pages by adding the correct tags on each of the pages.

Not everyone who owns a business may be well versed with JavaScript or know how to use it. Using it to create your site can only benefit your site because of the various aspects that JavaScript can add to it. Hence, it would always be helpful if you can hire a professional web design company who can help you build your site using JavaScript. The team of professional designers can sit with you, understand your business and design a site keeping all your business needs in mind.

© **Brian Draper**

45784238R00054

Made in the USA
San Bernardino, CA
17 February 2017